# A Cardiff chase

Mit Illustrationen von Karen Donnelly

**Dein Buch findest du auch in der Cornelsen Lernen App.**
Siehst du dieses Symbol in deinem Buch, findest du in deiner App
🔊 ein **Audio** (das Kapitel als Hörtext oder ein Lied).

**A Cardiff chase**

Lektüre zu Lighthouse 3

*Erarbeitet von:* Rebecca Robb Benne, Kopenhagen und Zoe Thorne, Royston
*Komposition 'A song about Wales':* Zoe Thorne
*unter beratender Mitwirkung von:* Nikolas Grote, Hannover
*in Zusammenarbeit mit der Englischredaktion:* Klaus Unger (Projektleitung), Stella Hunger und Chiara Castellano (verantwortliche Redakteurinnen) sowie Julian Theo Wacker
*Illustrationen:* Karen Donnelly, Brighton
*Tonstudio:* Clarity Studio Berlin
*Regie und Aufnahmeleitung:* Susanne Kreutzer, Berlin
*Tontechnik:* Dimitris Kritikos, Berlin
*Umschlagkonzept und -gestaltung:* Cornelsen Verlag Design / Rosendahl Berlin
*Layoutkonzept:* Klein & Halm, Berlin
*Layout und technische Umsetzung:* PER MEDIEN & MARKETING GmbH, Braunschweig

**www.cornelsen.de**

1. Auflage, 1. Druck 2025

Alle Drucke dieser Auflage sind inhaltlich unverändert und können im Unterricht nebeneinander verwendet werden.

Druck: H. Heenemann, Berlin

ISBN 978-3-06-036652-1

PEFC-zertifiziert
Dieses Produkt stammt aus nachhaltig bewirtschafteten Wäldern
PEFC/04-31-1156    www.pefc.de

# Contents

# Characters in the book

Owen Thomas is from Llandudno in North Wales. He speaks Welsh at home with his parents and he sings in the choir in Welsh too.

Dylan Jones is Owen's best friend in Llandudno. When he isn't playing rugby, he's always on his phone.

Glenys and Gareth Thomas are Owen's grandparents. They live in Cardiff.

Bronwyn is a very confident girl – and she thinks she's much cleverer than Owen and Dylan. Unfortunately, she doesn't care too much about fair play.

This story all starts with the Cardiff Angel and her exciting idea. But who is she? Read carefully and find out!

'It's great to be on holiday!' said Owen and smiled happily from the sofa. 'Yes, it is!' answered his friend Dylan. 'It's so kind of your grandparents to let me stay at their house with you. I'm really looking forward to seeing everything in Cardiff!'

'It's a great place,' said Owen. 'It isn't a big international capital city like London. I went to London once with my mum and dad and it was amazing – but there were so many people!'

'I like our town!' said Dylan. 'Llandudno is small, but it's cool. I miss the beach and the sea already!'

'Well, there isn't really a beach in Cardiff, but there's a fake beach near the Bay – near the water,' answered Owen. 'It's called Cardiff Bay Beach. There's some sand and some small pools. And there's a roller coaster and some other rides too.'

'Sounds fun,' said Dylan. 'I'll check it out on my phone.'

You just want to go on social media and check the latest comments from your followers!

'Oh please,' said Dylan. 'Just because you don't use social media much, that doesn't mean I can't have an online life.'

'Ha ha,' joked Owen. 'Be nice or I'll unfollow you!'

Dylan typed 'Cardiff Bay Beach' on his phone. He looked at the photos and skimmed the information quickly. 'Yeah, it looks cool,' he said. 'Oh, that's strange ...'

'What?' said Owen.

Dylan looked puzzled. 'Something has appeared on the page. It's a video. Something about a competition.'

'What? Don't tap on it!' said Owen. 'It's probably something nasty!'

'No, it's OK. It's an official Cardiff City video.' Dylan tapped on the link.

The video started playing and a strange voice started speaking.
'What's that?' asked Owen. 'Is it a voice-over? It sounds weird.'
'No, it's a woman,' said Dylan. 'But she's sitting in the dark so you can't
see her face. And there's some sort of filter on her voice so it sounds like
a computer.'
'Scary!' said Owen. 'What's it about?'
Dylan stopped the video, then sat down on the sofa next to Owen and
pressed PLAY again.

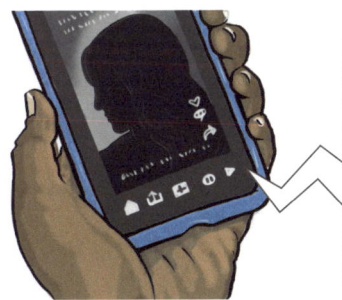

*Hello everyone, I'm the Cardiff Angel.
I've made this video to tell you about
a competition which has an amazing
prize. It's a competition for young
people between thirteen and eighteen
years old who live in Cardiff or have
family in Cardiff ...*

'Hey, that's us!' said Owen excitedly. 'We can do this! What do you think
the prize is?'
'Owen, please just watch and listen and then we might find out!' said
Dylan.

*The person or people – it can be
a pair or group of friends – who
win the competition will win a lot
of money. Enough money so that
you can follow your dreams!*

Wow!

'But why is she giving this money away?' asked Owen. 'Who is the
Cardiff Angel? Why isn't she using her real name? And why can't we see
her face?'
Dylan sighed. 'Please listen, Owen!'

*To begin with, let me say why I'm doing this. It's simple. I have a lot of money and I'd like to help somebody. At the same time, I'd like to turn the spotlight on my wonderful home city Cardiff. If you want to take part, you just have to solve a simple word puzzle. The puzzle is at the end of this video and the answer will give you the name of an AR app.*

'What's AR?' asked Owen. 'AR is the abbreviation for Augmented Reality,' answered Dylan. 'It means the app can show you digital images when you look at something through the camera on your phone.'
'Oh. That's cool!'

*Download the app from an app store, write your name or names and agree to the terms. Then just follow the clues! Good luck!*

*Teatime! What are you boys doing?*

*There's a competition in Cardiff. You can win lots of money! Can we do it please? Please?*

*Please, Mr and Mrs Thomas!*

'Let me see that,' said Mr Thomas. He took the phone and watched the video. 'Hmm, it seems to be real.' He checked on another website. 'Yes, look there's an article in our local paper about it.'
'It sounds hard,' said Mrs Thomas. 'Do you think you can do it?'
'Sure,' said Owen. 'Dylan is really good at tech and online things and I'm super clever at everything else.'
His grandma laughed. 'Well, OK,' she said. 'Good luck, boys!'
Owen and Dylan each took a cup of tea and looked at the word puzzle.

**1** **Can you help Owen and Dylan solve the Cardiff Angel's puzzle?**
Find the name of the app: Correct the words with the wrong spelling.
Then, circle the words with the correct spelling and write down the
name of the app.

capitel     dreem     sozial media

secret     simpel     voise     competetion

anser     prize     freind

App name: _____

**2** **BONUS PUZZLE: A strange subtitle**
Write the subtitle in the correct way.
Then write the correct letter from the
subtitle.

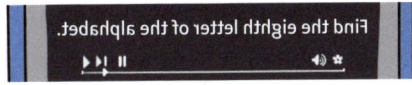

**!**

**Bonus puzzle:**
Collect a letter from the bonus
puzzle in each chapter.
Then write the letters in the
same order in Chapter 9 and
find a secret message.

_____

_____

Bonus letter: _____

**Who is the Cardiff Angel?**

In each chapter, there's some information about the
Cardiff Angel.
Write notes about the Cardiff Angel at the end of each
chapter on pages 53–56.

Owen's grandparents said it was OK for the boys to install the app on their phones and they set it up with their names. The first clue was already there!

In my first job I counted lots of money. It wasn't mine, but I knew that one day I'd have a million.

'Where do you have lots of money that isn't yours?' said Dylan. 'Oh, I know! Maybe she worked in a bank.'

'Mmm,' said Owen. 'Possible. But look at the picture. What does that look like to you?'

'Oh,' said Dylan. 'It's one of those arcade machines that are like a waterfall. You put two pence in and if you're lucky, the other coins fall over the edge.'

'If you're lucky!' said Owen. 'I never win!'

'Are there amusement arcades in Cardiff?' asked Dylan.

'Yes, there are,' said Owen. 'So the Angel worked in an arcade! But what do you think the 'bingo' card means? Did she win her money at bingo?'

'You can't win a million at bingo!' said Dylan.

'You usually win some cheap sunglasses or a toy donkey!'

'Or,' said Owen excitedly, 'maybe you can play bingo at one of the amusement arcades?'

'Yes! I'll look online,' said Dylan. 'Just a minute ... here it is. There's only one arcade with bingo.'

Owen and Dylan told Mr and Mrs Thomas where they were going and cycled to the amusement arcade.

'Look, there's the bingo!' said Dylan.

'And there are the machines. Come on!' called Owen.

'I'm just going to check in on the app,' said Dylan. 'Remember we have to do that, so the Angel knows we're at each place. ... OK, I've done it.'

Dylan looked up from his phone. A girl near them with brown hair suddenly looked away. Dylan smiled. 'I think that girl likes me,' he said to Owen.

Owen laughed. 'She's probably in the competition. And her name's Bronwyn,' he said to his surprised friend. 'She's wearing a necklace that spells her name,' he explained.

There were a lot of other teenagers in the arcade. A girl and a boy with phones in their hands put some coins in one of the machines. Nothing fell out and they looked disappointed. Then the boy looked around and hit the machine really hard.

'Hey, you,' shouted a guard in a blue uniform. 'Stop that!'

The boy laughed and hit the machine again. Another guard came over. 'OK, out you two!' she said. They followed the kids to the doors.

'Cool,' said Dylan. 'I saw they had the competition app on their phones. So two kids are out of the competition already!'

Owen and Dylan looked at the waterfall machines. There were lots of two-pence coins, some toys and some yellow plastic balls.

'This machine is good,' said Owen. 'It has a lot of coins near the edge. And you can win a watch!'

'I don't need a watch,' said Dylan. 'I use my phone for the time. And it isn't a smartwatch, it's just a cheap one.'

'Oh, Dylan, I actually think it's this machine here,' said Owen. 'It has … Wait. I think that Bronwyn girl is listening.'

Dylan went over to the girl, but she just looked at him without a word and walked away.

'I think we need to be careful of her,' Dylan said to Owen. 'She seems really smart.'

When Bronwyn was gone, Owen showed Dylan something in the machine. 'Look at that,' he said. There was a yellow plastic ball near the edge. And it had a message on it.

Owen and Dylan exchanged a pound for fifty two-pence coins and started to put them in the machine. Nothing moved. 'I think they put glue on these coins,' joked Dylan. He put in some more two-pence pieces and a few coins fell out, but the ball didn't move and stayed near the edge. Owen put more coins in. Nothing.

Dylan studied the machine carefully and put in the next coin in a different way. It went slowly to the side and pushed some coins over the top edge ... which pushed some other coins ... which pushed the plastic ball ... which moved ... and fell out! 'There you go, Owen,' he said proudly.

Dylan took the ball out of the machine. He was going to open it, but Owen put his hand on Dylan's arm. 'Not here,' he said quietly. Bronwyn was near them again and her green eyes were on the ball in Dylan's hand. 'Let's go a little further away from her,' said Owen. 'Over there.' Owen watched out for Bronwyn while Dylan took a piece of paper out of the ball and read it. 'It's a message from the Angel,' he said.

## 1 The secret message in the ball

Read the message and highlight the first letter of every fifth word.
Then write all the letters in the boxes in the same order.

Let me tell you something about myself. I like eating salad and noodles and cake, but I don't like rice. At the weekend I enjoy watching films on my tablet and I love video games. I have a big apartment and I like to relax at home when I don't have to work. What else? Well, I don't like nasty, mean people or bullies. If you're clever, polite and nice, you might maybe win the prize. But if you're horrible, this Cardiff competition won't end the way you want! Stay calm, be patient and kind, and remember to do your very best. Good luck!

☐☐☐☐☐☐☐ ☐☐☐☐☐☐ ☐☐ ☐☐☐ ☐☐☐

## 2 BONUS PUZZLE: Special bingo calls in the UK

a) **Choose the correct numbers from the box.**
**(There are three extra numbers.) Do the sum.**

1 · 2 · 3 · 4 · 13 ·
14 · 15 · 45 · 55

1 All the fives
2 Valentine's Day
3 Unlucky for some

4 Knock at the door (Tip: rhyme!)
5 Cup of tea (Tip: rhyme!)
6 One little duck

b) **What letter is the answer in the alphabet?**

Bonus letter: _____

Remember!

As Owen and Dylan left the amusement arcade and went to get their bikes, Bronwyn was just behind them. Suddenly she fell – but luckily Owen caught her.

Bronwyn ran off quickly.
'She was really unfriendly!' said Dylan.
'Yes, she was,' said Owen. Suddenly he thought about something.
He put his hand in his pocket – the yellow plastic ball from the machine was missing. Bronwyn had the clue!
'I told you she was smart,' said Dylan.

The two boys cycled from the amusement arcade to Cardiff Castle (Castell Caerdydd in Welsh). Inside there was a notice board with a list of the prices.
'Oh no, it costs £3 to go in!' said Dylan disappointedly. 'What are we going to do?'

'No problem,' said Owen. 'Grandad gave me some money.'
'But look at this notice! It says that you have to be part of a castle tour to visit the roof garden.'
'Well, we'll just have to join a group!' said Owen. 'This way!'
Owen and Dylan went upstairs to the top of Bute Tower. In front of them was an exchange class from France. The boys followed them into the roof garden and stood next to a friendly exchange student in a green cardigan.

Dylan checked in on the app. Suddenly his camera switched itself on!
'If we point it at the right thing, it'll show us an image or a message,' said Dylan to Owen.
'How about the fountain?' asked Owen. But before they could move closer to the fountain, a tall boy with his phone in his hand pushed them away impatiently and ran in front of them. 'I'm going to get the clue first!' he shouted.
'Oh no, this isn't going to end well!' said Dylan. 'Be careful!' he shouted. It was too late. The boy couldn't stop quickly enough. He hit his foot on the metal fountain and there was a nasty noise.
'Ow ow,' shouted the boy and touched his foot.
'I think it's broken!'
The guide from the group hurried over to the boy. 'Shall I get you some help?' he offered and helped the boy out of the room.
'I hope he's OK,' said Owen worriedly.
'Me too. But it's one more kid out of the competition!' said Dylan happily.

Dylan pointed his phone at the fountain, but nothing happened. Then he saw the statue. It was a mother and child, and the mother had a white headpiece. 'Look at that,' he said to Owen. 'Maybe the Cardiff Angel put the headpiece there as a clue.'

'I think you're right,' said Owen. 'I guess the headpiece is hers and she got married here, in this room.'

'And she has a daughter or a son,' said Dylan. 'Like the mother from the statue. Shall I try?'

He pointed his phone at the statue.

Dylan caught his breath when he saw the image on his phone. Owen caught his breath too when he saw it.

And when she came quietly into the room, pointed her phone at the statue and saw the amazing image on her screen, Bronwyn caught her breath too.

I don't understand. Why is the dragon wearing a waistcoat? And why has it got those cards?

## 1  The cards

Look at the dragon's playing cards.
Write the letters from the cards in the correct
order to find the next place.

## 2  BONUS PUZZLE: A quiz question

a) Answer this quiz question.
(TIP: use the tip box for help.
You can also find the answer in this
chapter.)

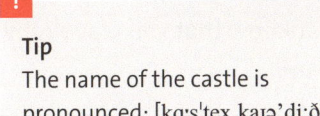

**!**

**Tip**
The name of the castle is
pronounced: [kɑːsˈtex kaɪəˈdiːð].

What is the name of Cardiff Castle in Welsh?

A   Castell Caerffili
B   Castell Caernarfon
C   Castell Caerdydd

The name is _____.

b) The bonus letter is the thirteenth letter of the correct answer in a).

Bonus letter: _____

Remember!

# 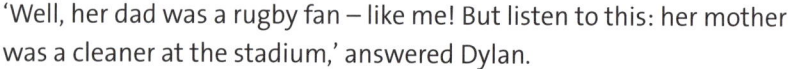 Chapter 4: A different kind of game

Owen and Dylan put the answer in the app and a few minutes later, a message with a programme and digital tickets for a rugby match for that afternoon appeared on the phone.

'Wow!' said Owen. 'The Angel must know that you play rugby, Dylan!'

'No, it's not that. In the message, she says that it's a special place for her.'

'Why?' asked Owen.

'Well, her dad was a rugby fan — like me! But listen to this: her mother was a cleaner at the stadium,' answered Dylan.

'Hmm,' said Owen. 'So the Angel's family wasn't rich. That means, she's made her money herself through hard work.'

'Yes, I'm curious about what her job is. Maybe she has her own business?' guessed Owen.

'Yes, maybe it has something to do with social media. Or maybe she has a well-being business. You can earn a lot of money with that.'

'Hmm,' answered Owen. 'If we can find out what her job is, we can find out who the Angel is.'

'True. But Owen, we have to go to the stadium now so we don't miss the match! I'm so excited. Wales versus England!'

Of course they are!

Wales are going to win, of course!

In the stadium before the match, Dylan and Owen checked in on the app and then watched the cheerleaders and their amazing gymnastics. Everywhere there were Welsh flags with red dragons on them!
Dylan pointed his phone at one, but nothing happened.
'It isn't the flag,' he said.
'No,' said Owen. 'Remember the dragon in the AR image had a waistcoat.'
'Maybe it's part of a video game,' said Dylan. 'Or maybe it's a cosplay dragon? But why are we at the game?'
'Let's just watch the game and see what happens,' said Owen. 'Listen to the Welsh players singing. I love the melody of the Welsh song.'

After an exciting first half, Owen and Dylan talked about the game.
'14-3 to Wales,' said Dylan. 'We can't lose!'
'Yeah, Wales is the best team! ... Oh, look, Dylan! That's it!'
'What?' asked Dylan. 'Oh yes! Let's go!'
The two boys ran down the stairs.
'Faster, Dylan!' said Owen. 'Do you see that girl next to the dragon? I saw her at Cardiff Castle!'

The girl shouted at the mascot angrily and two security guards quickly appeared and took her away.

Owen went up to the dragon and asked it very politely. 'Excuse me, Dragon. Could I please get the Angel's clue?'

'Of course, young man,' said the dragon. It whispered a private message in Owen's ear and Owen smiled.

Dylan looked at Owen excitedly. 'What did the dragon say?'
'It said that we'll see ourselves and we should watch very carefully. If we're clever, we'll get a message.'
'OK,' said Dylan. 'But what did it mean, see ourselves?'
'It probably means on the big screens in the stadium – you know, where they show pictures of the fans!'
'Of course! You're so clever, Owen. Let's go back to our seats.'

It was fifteen minutes to the end of the game. The Welsh fans waved their flags and sang loudly as well.
'I've watched the screens,' said Owen. 'But I haven't seen our picture. Do you think we've missed it?'
'Maybe the Angel wants us to watch the match? Come on Wales!'
'Well, it *is* a great match,' said Owen. '28 to 8. Sorry, England!'
'Owen, Owen, there we are!' shouted Dylan excitedly. 'On the screen! And now there's a code. But there are also lights and some sounds.'
'It's Morse code,' said Owen. 'You just need to connect the code to the correct letters.'
'But how do we do that?' asked Dylan.
'I know Morse code,' said Owen. 'Easy!'

## 1 A puzzle in a famous code

🔊 Look at the code below and listen.
Then look at the key for each letter/sound and write the two words.

| A | B | C | D | E | F | G | H | I | J | K | L | M |
|---|---|---|---|---|---|---|---|---|---|---|---|---|
| ·— | —··· | —·—· | —·· | · | ··—· | ——· | ···· | ·· | ·——— | —·— | ·—·· | —— |

| N | O | P | Q | R | S | T | U | V | W | X | Y | Z |
|---|---|---|---|---|---|---|---|---|---|---|---|---|
| —· | ——— | ·——· | ——·— | ·—· | ··· | — | ··— | ···— | ·—— | —··— | —·—— | ——·· |

The two words are _____.

## 2 BONUS PUZZLE: Pompom puzzle

a) Look at the letters on the cheerleaders' pompoms. Put the letters in the right order to find three words with 4/2/5 letters.
Write them in the boxes below.

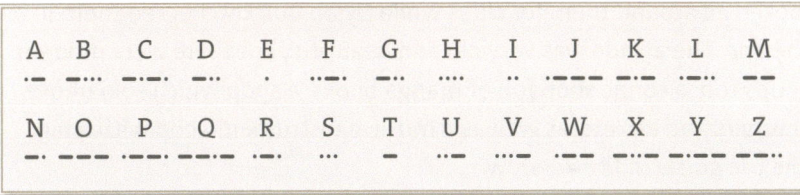

b) Write the letter from the blue box.

Bonus letter: _____

Remember!

'Come on, let's go!' said Owen. 'But there's still five minutes of the match to go!' said Dylan, looking shocked.

'Who cares? We can't waste time watching sport! We have to find clues!'

The boys went to find their bikes outside the stadium. Dylan still wasn't happy, but he soon felt better as they started cycling and he thought about the prize.

But Wales are winning!

They locked their bikes outside the shopping arcade, walked inside and looked all around them for clues while Dylan quickly checked them in on the app. The arcade was very old and beautiful, but there were modern shops too: a comic shop full of manga books, a shop which sold phone chargers and tablets, as well as a musical instrument shop with a big electric guitar in the window.

What do we do now?

Normally, Owen was good at finding clues and solving puzzles, but for once, he didn't have any ideas.

Then Dylan noticed a boy about their age. The boy looked at a shop and swiped something on his phone.

'I bet he's doing the competition too!' whispered Dylan to Owen. 'Oh look!'

Excuse me, can you please tell me where …

Go away! I don't have time for this!

'Well, that's not very polite!' whispered Owen. He walked over to the tourist and asked politely, 'Hi, would you like me to help?'

'Yes, please!' smiled the tourist and he showed the boys a screenshot of a map on his phone. 'I'm looking for this bookshop so I can buy a book about the history of coal mining in Cardiff. But I don't understand this map!'

Dylan and Owen looked at the map, but the screenshot on the tourist's phone wasn't very good, so Dylan looked up the bookshop on his instead.

'There it is!' he said, pointing to a shop on the corner. 'I hope you can find your book!'

The tourist smiled.

Thank you for helping me! And now I have something to tell you – I'm actually part of the competition!

'I'm sorry I lied to you,' said the tourist, 'but the Cardiff Angel wants only kind people to win the prize, so I had to check. But here's the truth: I already knew where the bookshop was. And before it was a bookshop, it was an electronics shop.'

'When she was young, the Cardiff Angel was very poor. Her dad died in an accident in the coal mine and her mum brought her up alone, but they had no money. The Angel loved computers and she was jealous of her friends who could buy one.'

'One day, she was in the shop, but she couldn't see anyone else. And she thought 'Maybe I can steal a computer! No one will ever know.' But the owner saw her and she was scared and very sorry.'

'Luckily, the man was kind and he gave her a second chance. He told her 'You can work in my shop on Saturdays and one day you can buy it.' And she did – she saved up and bought that exact computer, which she used to learn to code. And thanks to that man, it became a positive experience in her life.'

'Now that you know the story,' said the tourist, 'I have a riddle for you.'

**1 Can you help Owen and Dylan solve the riddle?**

Read the rhyme and write the seven letters in the boxes. Then write them down in the correct order. There's a clue to help you.

*One letter is in COMMENT and also once in SCHOOL.*  ⬜ 1

*One letter is third in EMOJI and one letter is first in TOOL.*  ⬜ 2 ⬜ 7

*One letter is silent in MINE and also loud in SEE.*  ⬜ 5

*One letter is in OURS, RUGBY and AGREE.*  ⬜ 6

*One letter is first in COMPUTER, another letter is in NOTE and SING. I'm something you'll go to if music is your thing!*  ⬜ 4 ⬜ 3

Secret word: _____

**2 BONUS PUZZLE: Different shops**

a) **Read the sentences and decide who has which shop. Make notes with the person's name and what they sell.**

1  Wyatt's shop sells shoes and is opposite shop A.
2  Ally's sports shop is next to Wyatt's.
3  Ty's clothes shop is between the music and the comic shop.
4  Liu's shop is on the left, next to the clothes shop.
5  Joe and Jan's shop sells comics and theirs is to the right of the clothes shop.
6  Ben's bookshop (which was an electronics shop) is next to a shop where you can buy things for judo, gymnastics and rugby.

b) **Write the letter for the bookshop.**

Bonus letter: _____

**Remember!**

*That's right! And one is going to start very soon, so take these tickets and go, quickly! You'll find the Cardiff Angel's most important gift there.*

The boys took the tickets and ran to get their bikes.

'The Cardiff Angel's most important gift must be the prize money!' said Dylan.

'The Wales Millennium Centre is a really big building, though,' said Owen. 'It's going to be difficult to find the money.'

When they arrived at the arts centre and checked in, there were lots of people around.

'I think there are lots of different events on today, not just our concert,' said Owen. 'Look at those people in costumes!' He pointed to a group of people with blue skin and enormous headpieces.

'They're characters from a TV series,' explained Dylan. 'There must be a big cosplay event today. People cut material and sew their own costumes – aren't they cool? And look over there at those people with signs!'

*Did you know that one in five teens is a victim of cyberbullying? Subscribe to our channel and help us change this terrible statistic!*

Suddenly, the boys noticed Bronwyn looking around the arts centre, while listening to a voice message on her phone.

'I'm surprised to see *her* here,' said Owen. 'Maybe she's not so bad if she helped the tourist too.'

'Hmm,' answered Dylan, who still had a pretty negative opinion of Bronwyn. 'Well, I can't see many other people who look like they're doing the competition now, which is good for us!'

Look! It's the dragon icon! Dylan, can you use your phone to scan the code?

Dylan held his phone up to the code and tapped the screen. A post on a social network opened up – but it was all in Welsh!

'I can read *some* of it, from the Welsh which I've learned at school,' said Dylan. 'But your Welsh is much better than mine.'

'*Mae hynny'n iawn* – that's right!' laughed Owen. 'But it's quite long ... Let me read it and sum it up.'

Owen read the post and mediated for Dylan. 'It says the Cardiff Angel's most important gift isn't money – it's her daughter, Bethany. She's a musician now and she's going to sing at the concert today.'

'There are four likes on the post,' said Dylan. 'So maybe there are only four of us who are doing the competition now? And look – Bronwyn has commented on it. You can see her profile picture there. It's a shame we can't delete the post before more people see it.'

'Dylan! That wouldn't be fair play!' said Owen.

Suddenly, they heard an announcement, but the connection wasn't very good and it kept breaking up.

'I think the concert is starting!' said Owen. 'Let's go and find our seats!'

Huh, and you thought maybe she wasn't so bad?!

The room went dark, but on the stage there was white, red and green lighting. A young woman with a guitar walked onto the stage as an exciting theme song from a film played and everyone in the audience clapped.

How are things, everyone? I'm so proud to be here today in our beautiful national arts centre and I hope you enjoy the concert. To start with, let's play a special song for our wonderful nation of Wales!

The band started playing their instruments and Dylan danced in his seat as Bethany sang. 'I love this!' he shouted to Owen. 'I can't stop moving – that rhythm is so cool!'

'Forget the rhythm!' answered Owen. 'Listen to the words – I think they're a clue!'

# Your turn

## 1 A song about Wales

Listen to the song and look at the list. Write the numbers that you hear in the correct boxes.

| | | | | | | | | | |
|---|---|---|---|---|---|---|---|---|---|
| 1 | un | 3 | tri | 5 | pump | 7 | saith | 9 | naw |
| 2 | dau | 4 | pedwar | 6 | chwech | 8 | wyth | 10 | deg |

**A**  `7`
**B**
**C**
**D**
**E**
**F**

The secret code is _____ .

## 2 BONUS PUZZLE: Secret letter puzzle

a) Complete the puzzle with words from this chapter.

1. something that you give to someone
2. something which you show to get into a concert or sports match
3. something that people wear to look like someone else
4. a website or app which you can use to talk to different people
5. something that you need so the audience can see people on stage
6. another word for a country
7. a person who comes from Wales is this

b) Write the letter from the blue box in a).

Bonus letter: _____

Remember!

'Well, we have the code,' said Owen. 'But what do we do with it?'
'I think there's something under my seat!' said Dylan.

*Quick, let's put in the code!*

Inside the box was a small picture of Techniquest, the big science museum in Cardiff.
'That's where we need to go next!' said Owen. 'Come on, let's go!'
The science museum wasn't far. The boys locked their bikes and ran inside, then checked in on the app.

'I haven't seen Bronwyn yet – maybe she didn't solve the clue!' said Dylan.

They looked around. There were all sorts of devices from the past up to the modern day: enormous machines that were the earliest computers, as well as typewriters, which people used before somebody invented the keyboard.

'Look at the keys!' said Dylan, pointing to a really old one. 'They're not in the same order as on a keyboard today. I bet it took a really long time to type out a document on that! And you couldn't edit it if you made a mistake.'

'Dylan, look at that notice on the wall!' said Owen suddenly.

THE SCIENCE MUSEUM WOULD LIKE TO THANK THE DRAGONTECH COMPANY FOR DONATING MANY OF THE DEVICES IN THIS EXHIBITION.

'There's the dragon symbol again!' said Dylan. 'I bet DragonTech is the Cardiff Angel's company. I've heard of it, but I don't know who the owner is.'

'Well, we know a bit more about the Cardiff Angel now, but we haven't found the next clue yet,' said Owen. 'Why don't we split up? I'll look on the first floor and you can look on this floor.'

'Sounds good,' answered Dylan. 'You have your phone, right? Get in touch if you find anything.'

Owen went upstairs and looked around. Up here, there was lots of old equipment from Cardiff's history: the original machines that people used to mine coal, devices from ships and more.

Dylan kept looking downstairs. There were some devices that visitors were allowed to try, like a special pair of colourful wireless headphones that changed colour when they played music. Dylan paired his phone with the headphones to see what they were like and listened happily as the lights flashed in time with the melody.

'This is all fun, but where's the next clue?' he thought. Then suddenly, he noticed a door with a symbol he recognized …

The door led to a small cupboard with some cleaning equipment and a cleaner's apron inside. It was dark in the cupboard, but even with the bad lighting, Dylan could see a poster on the wall.

Cardiff Bay, that must be the next place! Great, I'll find Owen.

But before he could leave, the door closed suddenly!
Dylan tried to push it open, but it was locked. Then he heard a laugh and he knew at once who the source of the problem was: Bronwyn.
"It's an annoying habit of yours, always following me about,' she called through the door. 'But this should stop you. That prize money is MINE!' She laughed again and ran away.
Dylan knocked on the door and shouted, but of course Owen couldn't hear him because he was upstairs. What could he do?
Then he remembered that Owen had his phone. Of course! He took a photo of the poster and forwarded it to Owen, then messaged him to explain the problem.

Good news – I know where we need to go next. But the bad news is that Bronwyn is here and she has locked me in a cupboard!

Oh no! I'll come and find you. Where are you?

It's the door with the dragon on it. I'll try to remember how I got here …

## 1 Rescue Dylan!

Look at the map and read Dylan's message to Owen.
Which door should Owen open?

*Go down the stairs, straight on past the phones and turn left before the tablets.
Take the second right, then left and it's the door opposite you.
Hurry up! Bronwyn has already left!*

Owen will find Dylan behind door _____.

## 2 BONUS PUZZLE: What's left?

a) In the box, cross out the tech words that are described in the sentences. Write the letter next to the correct description.

> **W** charger • **Y** emoji • **K** follower •
> **P** smartwatch • **C** troll • **R** voice-over

1 A small picture that is a symbol for something: _____

2 Someone who is horrible to people online: _____

3 A device which you can wear: _____

4 Someone who subscribes to your page or channel: _____

5 When you speak over a video: _____

b) Write the letter that you <u>didn't</u> cross out.

Bonus letter: _____

**Remember!**

There you are!

'Thanks Owen!' said Dylan as he came out of the cupboard.
'I can't believe she was so mean!' said Owen.
'Well, I'm not surprised,' answered Dylan. 'But look, while I was in the cupboard, I found out who the Cardiff Angel is!'

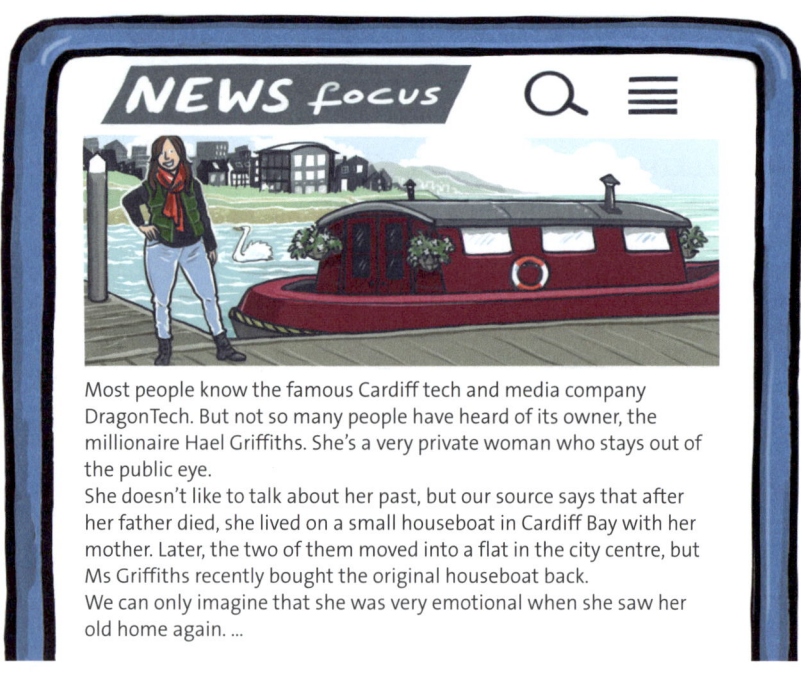

## NEWS *focus*

Most people know the famous Cardiff tech and media company DragonTech. But not so many people have heard of its owner, the millionaire Hael Griffiths. She's a very private woman who stays out of the public eye.
She doesn't like to talk about her past, but our source says that after her father died, she lived on a small houseboat in Cardiff Bay with her mother. Later, the two of them moved into a flat in the city centre, but Ms Griffiths recently bought the original houseboat back.
We can only imagine that she was very emotional when she saw her old home again. …

Dylan and Owen looked at each other. 'We need to find that houseboat,' said Owen. 'That must be where the prize money is!'

The boys cycled to the bay, checked in on the app and looked around. There were lots of houseboats in the flowing water, with numbers on each one.

'There are so many boats!' said Owen. 'And they all look very similar. How will we find the right one?'

'You won't!' said a nasty voice. Bronwyn was on a jetty over the water. 'I'll get there first!'

She started running along the jetty and looked at the boats. Dylan and Owen did the same, but they couldn't find any clues anywhere. No dragon symbols, just lots and lots of numbers.

'This is stupid!' shouted Owen finally. He turned to Bronwyn. 'Look, this doesn't have to be a competition. We're just as fast and as clever as you are. We've all worked hard to get this far. Why don't we work together? We all deserve some of the money. We can share it between us.'

Dylan didn't like the sound of this, but Bronwyn seemed to debate the idea for a moment.

'OK,' she said finally. 'That's a good idea. You must be pretty smart too. Come over here onto the jetty – I think I'm close.'

Dylan and Owen walked carefully along the wet jetty. But as they got close to Bronwyn ...

35

Dylan and Owen were shocked and nearly fell into the water, but then Bronwyn fell over a rope and suddenly ...

She waved her arms and shouted angrily from the cold water of the bay. 'Well, you tried to trick us!' shouted Dylan. But Owen looked worried. 'I think we should help her,' he said. 'What if she can't swim?' 'Seriously?!' asked Dylan. 'After all the horrible things that she did?' But then he looked at Owen's face and sighed. 'Fine ...'

'Look, she's safe. And someone from one of the other boats is coming to help her. Can we go now?' asked Dylan.
'Yes – we'll still get to the prize money first, don't worry!' answered Owen happily.
Suddenly, Dylan's phone made a noise and he looked at it. 'I need to charge my phone soon because the battery is almost dead. Look! There's a message from the app!'
The boys read the message.

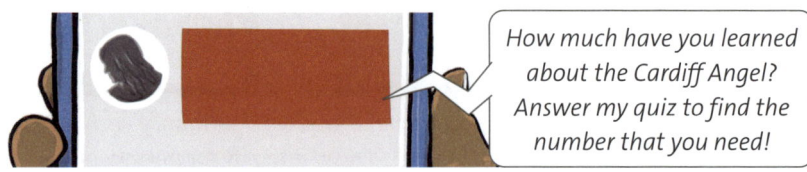

*How much have you learned about the Cardiff Angel? Answer my quiz to find the number that you need!*

## 1 Do the Angel's quiz!

Look at your notes about the Cardiff Angel. Answer the questions and write the numbers in the boxes. Then add the numbers together.

**A** Where was the Cardiff Angel's first job?

|   |   |   |   |
|---|---|---|---|
| **3** | in a shopping arcade | **5** | at the stadium |
| **7** | at an amusement arcade | **8** | at a restaurant |

**B** Where did her father work before he died?

|   |   |   |   |
|---|---|---|---|
| **12** | at Cardiff Castle | **11** | in a coal mine |
| **9** | in an electronics shop | **15** | at the science museum |

**C** Why was the Cardiff Angel grateful to a shop owner?

|   |   |   |   |
|---|---|---|---|
| **6** | He gave her a computer. | **10** | He taught her to code. |
| **4** | He was kind and didn't tell the police. | **3** | He married her. |

**D** Which of these isn't true?

|   |   |   |   |
|---|---|---|---|
| **1** | The Cardiff Angel had a child. | **6** | The Cardiff Angel became very rich. |
| **5** | The Cardiff Angel's mum was a teacher. | **2** | The Cardiff Angel gave devices to a museum. |

The houseboat number is ☐A + ☐B + ☐C + ☐D = _____ .

## 2 BONUS PUZZLE: More houseboat numbers

**a)** Look at the houseboats and solve the puzzle.

roller coaster ____ + rugby ____ + watch ____ – gymnast ____ = _____

**b)** What letter of the alphabet is the answer?

Bonus letter: _____

**Remember!**

'That's it!' shouted Dylan happily. 'We have the number, so we just need to find the boat!'

They could hear Bronwyn shouting angrily as someone tried to help her out of the water when they saw the houseboat with the number that they were looking for.

*It isn't locked! We've found it!*

They went inside the boat and looked around. 'It must be here somewhere!' said Owen. 'Come on, let's look.'

Can you find the prize money?

The boys opened the dragon suitcase. Inside it was more money than they had ever seen in their life! They couldn't believe it!
Dylan and Owen looked at each other, their mouths open.
'We won!'
Suddenly, there was a tap on the window and the boys turned to see a face looking at them – the Cardiff Angel!

I'm so happy that you two won the prize money. You seem like very kind boys. Come on, let's go and tell your families the good news.

Owen told Ms Griffiths how to get to his grandparents' house and she followed the two cycling boys in her large black car.
'They won't believe it when we tell them!' whispered Owen excitedly.
But when Mr Thomas opened the door, there was another surprise.

Gareth???

Hael? Is that really you?

Owen looked at them. 'How do you know each other? That's impossible!'

Mr Thomas smiled at his grandson. 'Owen, did I ever tell you that when I was a young man, I owned an electronics shop?'

*... and that's the whole story.*

Ms Griffiths smiled at Mr Thomas. 'How are things, Gareth? I'm so sorry we lost touch over the years. I always wanted to thank you, but I didn't know how to find you after you sold the shop. You changed my life.' She couldn't keep the emotion out of her voice. 'I nearly stole that computer ...'

Mr Thomas shook his head. 'I could see you were a good person really and I'm so happy that you found a better way. Look at all the wonderful things that you've done with your skills and your money! That's the best kind of thank you. But I'm not surprised. Your name, Hael, does mean 'kind' in Welsh.'

'Well, that's why I wanted to do this competition, to help a young person in Cardiff to find a better life – in the way that you helped me. So it's perfect that your grandson and his best friend are the winners! Let's keep in touch now.' Then she turned to Dylan and Owen.

*Now, boys, you have an important choice. This is a lot of money and you have to find the best way to use it. So I have one last thing to ask you. I want you to spend some money, save some and share some.*

*Maybe we could give some money to Bronwyn, so she can go on her class trip!*

## 1  The prize money

a) Write what you think Owen and Dylan will do with the money. You can use the ideas in the box to help you, or your own ideas.

> buy / save for [a new phone / a computer / a present / ...]
> give some money to [charity / school / family / Bronwyn / ...]
> pay for [a holiday / a coding course / a concert / ...]

*I'm going to:*

SPEND  _____

SAVE  _____

SHARE  _____

*I'm going to:*

SPEND  _____

SAVE  _____

SHARE  _____

b) Write your own ideas for how YOU would use the prize money.

|  | SPEND | _____ |
| --- | --- | --- |
| *I would:* | SAVE | _____ |
|  | SHARE | _____ |

## 2  BONUS PUZZLE: The secret message

a) Write the bonus letters from each chapter in the boxes. They spell a secret message in Welsh. If you're not sure if you have found all the letters, the message is also hidden in two pictures in chapter 9.

☐☐☐☐  ☐☐☐☐

b) Find the meaning of the secret message online!

# Vocabulary

Das chronologische **Vocabulary** kannst du nutzen, wenn du wissen möchtest, was ein englisches Wort bedeutet, wie man es ausspricht oder wie es geschrieben wird.

Die Vokabeln im Vocabulary sind farblich unterschiedlich gekennzeichnet:

**rugby** (blau)         Lernwortschatz aus Lighthouse 3, Unit 4
**angel** (schwarz)      neue Vokabel, die nicht in Lighthouse 3 vorkommt
**filter** (grau)        Vokabel aus Lighthouse 3, die kein Lernwortschatz ist

### Abkürzungen

*infml*              *informal* (umgangssprachlich)
*jd. / jn. / jm.*    jemand / jemanden / jemandem
*p.*                 *page* (Seite)
*pl.*                *plural* (Mehrzahl)
*sb.*                *somebody* (jemand, jemanden, jemandem)
*sth.*               *something* (etwas)

## Cast list

### p. 4

**choir** ['kwaɪə] der Chor
**rugby** ['rʌgbi] das Rugby *(Ballsportart)*

### p. 5

**angel** ['eɪndʒl] der Engel

## Chapter 1

### p. 6

(to) **let** [let] **let, let** lassen
**international** [ɪntəˈnæʃnəl] international
**bay** [beɪ] die Bucht
**sand** [sænd] der Sand
**roller coaster** ['rəʊlə kəʊstə] die Achterbahn

**social media** [səʊʃl ˈmiːdiə] die sozialen Medien **social** sozial **media** *(pl)* die Medien
**latest** ['leɪtɪst] neueste/r/s, aktuelle/r/s
**comment** (about / on sth.) ['kɒment] der Kommentar (über / zu etwas) (to) **comment** (about / on sth.) (etwas) kommentieren
**follower** ['fɒləʊə] der/die Follower/in
(to) **unfollow** [ˌʌnˈfɒləʊ] entfolgen *(auf sozialen Medien nicht mehr folgen)*
(to) **type** (in) [taɪp] (ein-)tippen
(to) **skim** (a text) [skɪm] (einen Text) überfliegen *(um den Inhalt grob zu erfassen)*
(to) **tap** sth. [tæp] tippen an / auf etwas, (leise) klopfen **tap** das leise Klopfen

## p. 7

**voice** [vɔɪs]  die Stimme
**voice-over** ['vɔɪs əʊvə]
  der Filmkommentar, die Off-Stimme
**filter** ['fɪltə]  **1.** der Filter **2.** filtern
(to) **press** [pres]  drücken
**which** [wɪtʃ]  der/die/das, die *pl.*
  *(Relativpronomen für Dinge und
  Tiere)*
**who** [huː]  der/die/das, die *pl.*
  *(Relativpronomen für Personen)*

## p. 8

**To begin with, ...**  Zunächst (einmal)
  ..., Anfangs ...  **To start with, ...**
  *(Synonym)*
**simple** ['sɪmpl]  einfach
**abbreviation** (of / for)  [əbriːviˈeɪʃn]
  die Abkürzung (für)
**augmented reality (AR)**
  [ɔːɡˌmentɪd riˈæləti]  erweiterte
  Realität *(Technologie, die echte Bilder
  mit digitalen Bildern kombiniert)*
**image** ['ɪmɪdʒ]  das Bild,
  die Abbildung
(to) **agree to** sth.  [əˈɡriː]  in etwas
  einwilligen, einer Sache zustimmen
**terms** *(pl)*  [tɜːmz]
  die (Vertrags-)Bindungen,
  die Konditionen
**Good luck!** [ɡʊd lʌk]  Viel Glück!
**teatime** ['tiːtaɪm]  die Teestunde

## p. 9

**subtitle** ['sʌbtaɪtl]  der Untertitel

## Chapter 2

## p. 10

(to) **install** [ɪnˈstɔːl]  installieren,
  einbauen
(to) **set sth. up**  etwas einrichten,
  etwas aufbauen
**yours** [jɔːz]  deine, deiner, deins
  *(Possessivpronomen zu „you", auch:
  eurer, eure, eures)*
**amusement arcade**
  [əˈmjuːzmənt ɑːˈkeɪd]  die Spielhalle,
  der Spielsalon
**waterfall** ['wɔːtəfɔːl]  der Wasserfall
**edge** [edʒ]  der Rand, die Kante
**bingo** ['bɪŋɡəʊ]  das Bingo(-spiel)
**donkey** ['dɒŋki]  der Esel
**million** ['mɪljən]  die Million

## p. 11

**teenager** ['tiːneɪdʒə]  der Teenager
**watch** [wɒtʃ]  die Armbanduhr
  **smartwatch** ['smɑːtwɒtʃ]
  die Smartwatch
**actually** ['æktʃuəli]  tatsächlich,
  eigentlich
**without** [wɪˈðaʊt]  ohne

## p. 12

**There you go.**  Hier, bitte schön.
  *(auch:)* Da hast du's! / Na siehst du!

## p. 13

**rhyme** [raɪm]  der Reim
**cup** [kʌp]  die (Tee-)Tasse
**duck** [dʌk]  die Ente

## Chapter 3

**p. 14**

**roof** [ruːf]  das Dach
**roof garden**  der Dachgarten

**p. 15**

**notice** ['nəʊtɪs]  (be-)merken  **notice**
der Anschlag, die Bekanntmachung
**notice board**  das Schwarze Brett,
die Anschlagtafel
**exchange** [ɪks'tʃeɪndʒ]
der Schüleraustausch,
der Austausch, der Wechsel
**exchange class**  *Schulklasse, die am*
*Schüleraustausch teilnimmt*
**exchange student**
der/die Austauschschüler/in
**cardigan** ['kɑːdɪgən]  die Strickjacke
**Shall I ...?** [ʃæl], [ʃəl]  Soll ich ...?
(to) **offer** ['ɒfə]  (an-)bieten

**p. 16**

**headpiece** ['hedpiːs]
der Kopfschmuck
(to) **guess** [ges]  (er-)raten,
annehmen, vermuten
**hers** [hɜːz]  ihrer, ihre, ihres
*(Possessivpronomen zu „she")*
**breath** [breθ]  der Atem(-zug)
**waistcoat** ['weɪskəʊt]  die Weste

## Chapter 4

**p. 18**

**rich** [rɪtʃ]  reich
**well-being** ['wel biːɪŋ]
das Wohl(-ergehen)
**versus (v** or **vs)** ['vɜːsəs]  gegen
*(bei Wettkämpfen)*, gegenüber

**p. 19**

**cheerleader** ['tʃɪəliːdə]
der/die Cheerleader/in
**gymnastics** [dʒɪm'næstɪks]
die Gymnastik, das Turnen
**gymnast** ['dʒɪmnæst]
der/die Turner/in
**cosplay** ['kɒspleɪ]  das Cosplay
*(sich als eine Figur aus z. B. einem*
*Manga verkleiden)*
**melody** ['melədi]  die Melodie

**p. 20**

(to) **whisper** ['wɪspə]  flüstern
**private** ['praɪvət]  privat, persönlich
**... as well as ...** [əz 'wel əz]
sowohl ... als auch ...
(to) **connect (to / with)** [kə'nekt]
(sich) verbinden (mit)

**p. 21**

**pompom** ['pɒm pɒm]  der Pompon

## Chapter 5

### p. 22

**Who cares?** [keəz] Wen interessiert das? / Was soll's? / Na und?
**shopping arcade** [ˈʃɒpɪŋ ɑːkeɪd] die Einkaufspassage
**manga** [ˈmæŋgə] der Manga *(japanische Comicform)*
(to) **charge** [tʃɑːdʒ] aufladen
**charger** das Ladegerät
**tablet** [ˈtæblət] das Tablet *(Tablet-PC)*
**instrument** [ˈɪnstrəmənt] das Instrument
**normally** [ˈnɔːməli] normalerweise
**for once** ausnahmsweise, dieses eine Mal

### p. 23

**age** [eɪdʒ] das Alter, die Altersgruppe
(to) **swipe** [swaɪp] wischen *(auf Touchscreen)*, durchziehen, einlesen *(z. B. Kreditkarte)*
(to) **bet** [bet] wetten
**Would you like me to ...?** Möchtest du, dass ich ...?
**screenshot** [ˈskriːnʃɒt] der Screenshot *(Abbildung dessen, was auf einem Bildschirm zu sehen ist)*
**coal** [kəʊl] die Kohle
**mining** [ˈmaɪnɪŋ] der Bergbau
**mine** das Bergwerk
(to) **mine** sth. etwas abbauen, fördern
**his** [hɪz] seiner, seine, seins *(Possessivpronomen zu „he")*
**corner** [ˈkɔːnə] die Ecke

### p. 24

(to) **lie** (to sb.) [laɪ] (jn. an-)lügen
**truth** [truːθ] die Wahrheit
**jealous** (of) [ˈdʒeləs] neidisch (auf), eifersüchtig
**owner** [ˈəʊnə] der/die Besitzer/in
**exact** [ɪgˈzækt] genau, exakt
**positive** [ˈpɒzətɪv] positiv
**riddle** [ˈrɪdl] das Rätsel

### p. 25

**ours** [ɑːz], [ˈaʊəz] unserer, unsere, unseres *(Possessivpronomen zu „we")*
**mine** [maɪn] meine, meiner, meins *(Possessivpronomen zu „I")*
**emoji** [ɪˈməʊdʒi] das Emoji
**tool** [tuːl] das Werkzeug, das (Hilfs-)Mittel
**theirs** [ðeəz] ihrer, ihre, ihrs *(Possessivpronomen zu „they")*
**judo** [ˈdʒuːdəʊ] das Judo

## Chapter 6

### p. 26

**millenium** [mɪˈleniəm] das Jahrtausend
**skin** [skɪn] die Haut, die Schale *(z. B. Banane)*
**enormous** [ɪˈnɔːməs] riesig
**series** [ˈsɪəriːz] *pl.* **series** die Serie, die Sendereihe
(to) **cut** [kʌt] **cut, cut** schneiden
(to) **sew** [səʊ] **sewed, sewn** nähen
**troll** [trəʊl] der Troll *(Provokateur/in in Onlinemedien)*
**cyberbullying** [ˈsaɪbəbʊliːŋ] das Cybermobbing

one in five  eine/r von fünf(-en);
jede/r Fünfte
victim  ['vɪktɪm] das Opfer
(to) subscribe to sth.  [səb'skraɪb]
etwas abonnieren
channel  ['tʃænl] der Sender,
der (TV-)Kanal
statistic  [stə'tɪstɪk] die statistische
Tatsache / Größe

## p. 27

voice message  ['vɔɪs mesɪdʒ]
die Sprachnachricht
negative  ['negətɪv] negativ
icon  ['aɪkɒn] das Icon (Symbol auf
Bildschirm)
post  [pəʊst] der Post (Beitrag in
sozialen Medien)
network  ['netwɜːk] das Netz(-werk)
social network  das soziale Netzwerk
(to) sum sth. up  [sʌm 'ʌp]
etwas zusammenfassen
(to) mediate  ['miːdieɪt] vermitteln
(inhaltl. wiedergeben)
like  [laɪk] der Like („Gefällt mir" auf
sozialen Medien)
profile  ['prəʊfaɪl] das Profil
(to) delete  [dɪ'liːt] löschen

## p. 28

connection  [kə'nekʃn]
die Verbindung
(to) break up  zerbrechen,
zusammenbrechen
(Telefonverbindung)
stage  [steɪdʒ] die Bühne
lighting  ['laɪtɪŋ] die Beleuchtung

theme  [θiːm] das Thema
theme song  der Titelsong
How are things?  Wie geht's (so)?
national  ['næʃnəl] national
nation  ['neɪʃn] die Nation
rhythm  ['rɪðəm] der Rhythmus

## Chapter 7

## p. 30

device  [dɪ'vaɪs] das Gerät,
der Apparat
typewriter  ['taɪpraɪtə]
die Schreibmaschine
(to) invent  [ɪn'vent] erfinden
key  ['kiː] der Schlüssel, die Taste
keyboard  ['kiːbɔːd] die Tastatur
document  ['dɒkjumənt]
das Dokument, die Textdatei
(to) edit  ['edɪt] bearbeiten, editieren
exhibition  [,eksɪ'bɪʃn]
die Ausstellung

## p. 31

symbol  ['sɪmbl] das Symbol
(to) split up  (sich) trennen, aufteilen
(to) get in touch (with)  [tʌtʃ]
(sich) in Verbindung setzen (mit),
Kontakt aufnehmen (zu)
original  [ə'rɪdʒənl] original,
ursprünglich
ship  [ʃɪp] das Schiff
(to) debate  [dɪ'beɪt] debattieren,
diskutieren (über)
debate  die Debatte
(to) exchange  [ɪks'tʃeɪndʒ]
(aus-)tauschen

diary ['daɪəri] der Kalender,
das Tagebuch
wireless ['waɪələs] kabellos
(to) **pair** sth. (with sth.) [peə]
etwas (mit etwas) koppeln
(to) **flash** [flæʃ] blitzen, aufleuchten

## p. 32

**cupboard** ['kʌbəd] der Besenschrank
**apron** ['eɪprən] die (Koch-)Schürze
**source** [sɔːs] die Quelle
*(z. B. Webseite, Text)*
**habit** ['hæbɪt] die (An-)Gewohnheit
(to) **forward** sth. **to** sb. ['fɔːwəd]
etwas an jn. weiterleiten
(to) **message** sb. ['mesɪdʒ] jm. eine
(Text-)Nachricht schreiben

## Chapter 8

## p. 34

**millionaire** [ˌmɪljə'neə]
der/die Millionär/in
**houseboat** ['haʊsbəʊt] das Hausboot
**emotional** [ɪ'məʊʃənl] emotional
**emotion** [ɪ'məʊʃn] die Emotion

## p. 35

(to) **flow** [fləʊ] fließen, stömen
**flowing** fließend
**jetty** ['dʒeti] der Anlegesteg, der Pier
(to) **deserve** sth. [dɪ'zɜːv]
etwas verdienen
**wet** [wet] nass

## p. 36

**battery** ['bætəri] der Akku,
die Batterie

## Chapter 9

## p. 39

**suitcase** ['suːtkeɪs] der Koffer
**mouth** [maʊθ] der Mund

## p. 40

(to) **keep / stay in touch** (with) [tʌtʃ]
in Verbindung / Kontakt bleiben
(mit) (to) **lose touch** (with)
den Kontakt verlieren (mit)

# Answer key

Im **Answer key** kannst du nachschlagen, wenn du wissen möchtest, ob du die richtige Lösung gefunden hast oder welche weiteren Lösungen möglich sind.

## Chapter 1

**1  Can you help Owen and Dylan solve the Cardiff Angel's puzzle?**
**Correct spelling:**
capital, social media, simple, competition, dream, voice, answer, friend
**App name:** secret prize

**2  BONUS PUZZLE: A strange subtitle**
Find the eighth letter of the alphabet.
Bonus letter = *H*

## Chapter 2

**1  The secret message in the ball**
secret garden in the sky

**2  BONUS PUZZLE: Special bingo calls in the UK**
a) *55 − 14 − 13 − 4 − 3 + 2 = 23*
b) Bonus letter = *W*

## Chapter 3

**1  The cards**
S − T − A − D − I − U − M (stadium)

**2  BONUS PUZZLE: A quiz question**
a) The name is *C) Castell Caerdydd*.
b) Bonus letter = *Y*

# Chapter 4

## 1  A puzzle in a famous code

The two words are *shopping arcade*.

s    h    o    p    p    i    n    g      a    r    c    a    d    e

## 2  BONUS PUZZLE: Pompom puzzle

a)  Come on Wales
b)  Bonus letter = *L*


# Chapter 5

## 1  Can you help Owen and Dylan solve the riddle?

Secret word: *CONCERT*

## 2  BONUS PUZZLE: Different shops

a)

| *4* | *3* | *5* |
|-----|-----|-----|
| *Liu, music* | *Ty, clothes* | *Joe and Jan, comics* |

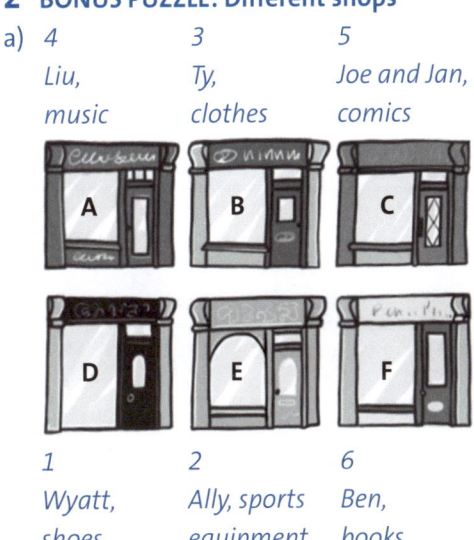

| *1* | *2* | *6* |
|-----|-----|-----|
| *Wyatt, shoes* | *Ally, sports equipment* | *Ben, books* |

b)  Bonus letter = *F*

# Chapter 6

## 1  A song about Wales

A  city: 7
C  dragon: 1
E  mountain: 6
B  language: 2
D  river: 3
F  Wales: 1

The secret code is *721361*.

## 2  BONUS PUZZLE: Secret letter puzzle

a)

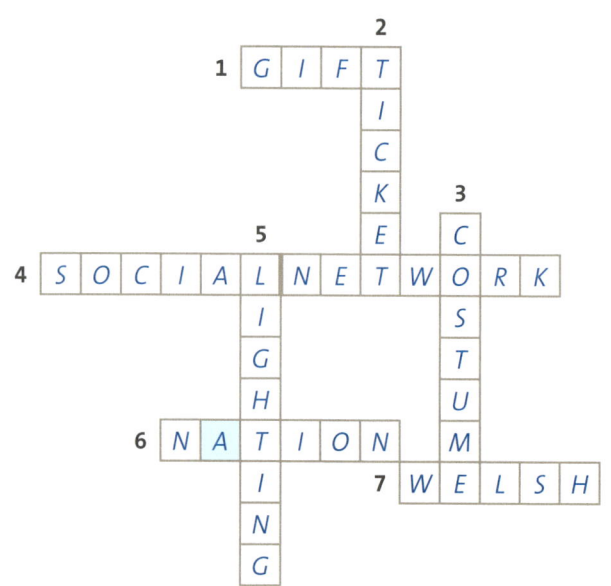

b)  Bonus letter = *A*

# Chapter 7

## 1 Rescue Dylan!

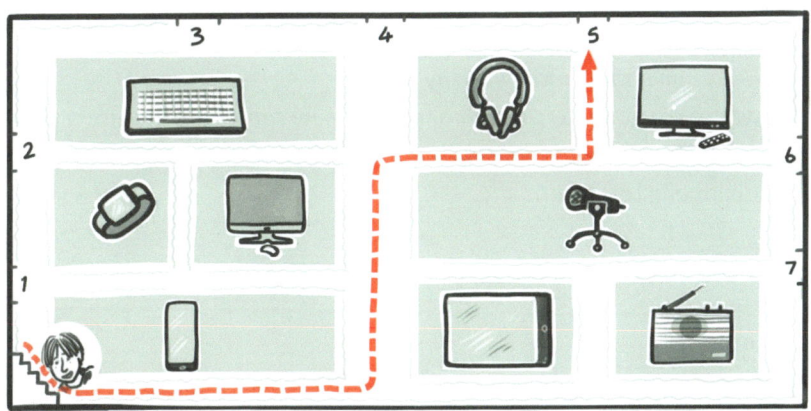

Owen will find Dylan behind door *5*.

## 2 BONUS PUZZLE: What's left?

a) 1 Y   2 C   3 P   4 K   5 R

b) Bonus letter = *W*

# Chapter 8

## 1 Do the Angel's quiz!

A 7   B 11   C 4   D 5

The houseboat number is *7 + 11 + 4 + 5 = 27*.

## 2 BONUS PUZZLE: More houseboat numbers

a) *7 + 8 + 6 − 3 = 18*

b) Bonus letter = *R*

# Chapter 9

## 1 The prize money
a) **Lösungsbeispiele:**

Dylan: I'm going to *buy a new computer, save for a new guitar and give some money to my family*.

Owen: I'm going to *spend money on a new computer, save for a trip to Paris and share with my choir*.

b) Individuelle Lösungen

## 2 BONUS PUZZLE: The secret message
a) Hwyl fawr
b) Goodbye